31 Days of WISDOM

A Journey Through the Heart of Proverbs

Aaron Montague, MBA, M.Div.

31 Days of Wisdom
A Journey Through the Heart of Proverbs

Kingdom Publishing, LLC
1350 Blair Drive, Suite F
Odenton, MD 21113

First printed in the USA

ISBN: 978-1-9670067-20-5 (paperback)
ISBN: 978-1-967006-21-2 (eBook)

Cover design by Kingdom Publishing, LLC.

DEDICATION

To My Mother, Jeannie Montague

This book is lovingly dedicated to the woman whose life is a living proverb — a tapestry woven with wisdom, love, and grace.

Mom, you have been my first teacher, my quiet intercessor, and the steadfast voice of faith in every season of my life. You walked before me in the trust and wisdom of the Lord, showing that true strength is clothed in humility and that peace is born from prayer.

Your life has been a sermon without words — preaching patience when storms raged, compassion when others faltered, and grace when it would have been easier to give up. Through you, I learned that wisdom isn't loud; it's steadfast. It's in the way you love, forgive, and believe — always.

I am forever grateful to God for the gift of you.

Your hands have shaped my faith, your prayers have covered my journey, and your example continues to guide my path.

You are, and always will be, the embodiment of wisdom walking — a crown of grace upon our family and a reflection of God's gentle strength in human form.

With everlasting love and gratitude,

Aaron

"Wisdom is the principal thing; therefore get wisdom: and with all thy getting get understanding."

— Proverbs 4:7 (KJV)

PREFACE

This book was birthed in the quiet places of reflection — in those sacred hours when Scripture becomes mirror, melody, and medicine. 31 Days of Wisdom is not simply a reading plan; it is a spiritual pilgrimage through the Proverbs — one day, one verse, one transformation at a time.

Each reflection begins with Scripture, flows through meditation, and concludes in prayer — because wisdom must touch both the mind and the heart. You will hear many voices here — my own and those of beloved friends and family — because wisdom was never meant to be walked alone. It is community made sacred by grace.

May every page draw you deeper into the knowledge of God, soften your spirit with understanding, and awaken the quiet courage to live what you learn.

Table of Contents

Introduction

Week One – The Fear of the Lord

Day 1: The Beginning of Knowledge 3
— Proverbs 1:7
Day 2: The Path of the Upright 5
— Proverbs 2:6–9
Day 3: Trust in the Lord with All Your Heart 7
— Proverbs 3:5–6
Day 4: Guard Your Heart with All Diligence 9
— Proverbs 4:23
Day 5: Wisdom Is the Principal Thing 11
— Proverbs 4:7
Day 6: Consider the Ant 14
— Proverbs 6:6
Day 7: The Pure Path 16
— Proverbs 7:2
End of Week Reflection 18

Week Two – The Path of Understanding

Day 8: The Whisper Beyond the Noise 21
— Proverbs 8:1–4
Day 9: The Fear of the Lord: True Wisdom Builds
a Stable Life 23
— Proverbs 9:10
Day 10: Integrity Is Quiet Strength 25
— Proverbs 10:9
Day 11: The Tongue of the Wise 27
— Proverbs 18:21

Day 12: The Law of Return 29
 — Proverbs 12:14
Day 13: The Waiting Saints: Hope Restored 31
 — Proverbs 13:12
Day 14: Wisdom Builds the House 33
 — Proverbs 14:1
End of Week Reflection 35

Week Three – The Heart of Trust

Day 15: The Power of Words 39
 — Proverbs 18:21
Day 16: Commit Your Plans to the Lord 41
 — Proverbs 16:3
Day 17: A Friend Loves at All Times 43
 — Proverbs 17:17
Day 18: The Name of the Lord Is a Strong Tower 45
 — Proverbs 18:10
Day 19: The Power of Patience 47
 — Proverbs 19:11
Day 20: The Glory of a King Is to Overlook a Matter 49
 — Proverbs 20:3
Day 21: The Righteous Are Bold as a Lion 51
 — Proverbs 28:1
End of Week Reflection 53

Week Four – The Way of Wisdom

Day 22: A Good Name Is Rather to Be Chosen Than
 Great Riches 57
 — Proverbs 22:1
Day 23: Humility Comes Before Honor 59
 — Proverbs 22:4

Day 24: The Rich and the Poor Meet Together 61
    — Proverbs 22:2
Day 25: He That Hath a Bountiful Eye Shall Be Blessed .. 63
    — Proverbs 22:9
Day 26: As a Man Thinketh in His Heart, So Is He 65
    — Proverbs 23:7
Day 27: As Iron Sharpens Iron 67
    — Proverbs 27:17
Day 28: Where There Is No Vision, the People Perish ... 69
    — Proverbs 29:18
End of Week Reflection 71

Week Five – The Rewards of Righteousness

Day 29: The Righteous Are as Bold as a Lion 75
    — Proverbs 28:1
Day 30: The Mouth of the Righteous Is a Well of Life 77
    — Proverbs 10:11
Day 31: The Faithful and Virtuous Woman 79
    — Proverbs 31:10
End of Week Reflection 81

Epilogue 85

Special Prayer — Forgiveness, Restoration, Renewal and
    Thanksgiving 87

About the Author 91

Introduction
The Beginning of Knowledge

— Proverbs 1:7
"The fear of the Lord is the beginning of knowledge: but fools despise wisdom and instruction."

Wisdom begins where pride ends — at the threshold of reverence. I once thought knowledge was information, but I have since learned that it is revelation. To fear the Lord is not to live in terror but to live in awe — to stand so aware of His holiness that all lesser pursuits fall away.

This journey through Proverbs is meant to be personal and practical. Let each day's reflection rest in your heart. Read slowly. Breathe deeply. And at the end of each prayer, listen — for wisdom always whispers before she shouts.

1

THE FEAR OF THE LORD

Day 1

The Beginning of Knowledge

Proverbs 1:7
"The fear of the Lord is the beginning of knowledge: but fools despise wisdom and instruction."

Reflection

I spent my entire youth as the fool who despised wisdom. I was devoid of understanding, deaf to instruction, and blind to consequence. Sinners enticed me, and I eagerly followed, imagining their voices were my own desires. I was that young sailor, led like an ox to the slaughter—drifting through life's currents without compass or conviction.

Someone once said, "God protects babies and fools," and I was surely that fool, preserved only by grace I did not deserve. But in time, the fear of the Lord seized me—not a polite reverence, but a trembling, soul-awakening fear that exposed my folly and invited me into surrender.

That fear became the doorway to wisdom. It was not book learning, nor surface knowledge, but a deep, experiential understanding born of repentance and yielding. The moment I bowed in awe before the Lord, I began to know Him—not through theory, but through encounter. That was the beginning of knowledge for me: when reverence replaced rebellion, and the God I once ignored became the God I could no longer live without.

Meditative Reflection

True wisdom begins not with answers, but with awareness — awareness that God is holy, life is sacred, and we are stewards of His grace. When awe replaces arrogance, knowledge takes root. Pause and breathe here. Let your spirit bow in quiet reverence. The fear of the Lord does not crush; it corrects. It does not enslave; it enlightens.

Affirmation Prayer

Adonai, my Teacher and my Truth,
Awaken in me the holy reverence that opens understanding.
Strip me of pride and make me teachable.
Let Your holiness humble my heart and Your mercy renew my mind.
May every lesson lead me nearer to Your presence and deeper into Your wisdom.
In the matchless Name of Yeshua, Amen.

Wisdom Key

Reverence is not restraint—it is revelation. To fear the Lord is to finally see clearly.

Day 2
The Path of the Upright

Proverbs 2:6–9

"For the Lord giveth wisdom: out of his mouth cometh knowledge and understanding. He layeth up sound wisdom for the righteous: he is a buckler to them that walk uprightly. He keepeth the paths of judgment, and preserveth the way of his saints."

Reflection

There comes a moment in every life when the eyes of the heart are opened, and the veil of ignorance is gently lifted by the Spirit of Truth. I look back now and realize that so much of what I once called "living" was nothing more than habit—patterns learned in darkness, choices born of blindness. Some were innocent, others harmful, but all were empty without wisdom.

When I began to truly fear the Lord—not with terror, but with reverent awe—my steps took on new direction. His counsel became my compass. His whisper became my wisdom. And though I had wandered through many dangers, toils, and snares, it was His grace that steadied my trembling feet.

Now, I see that every misstep was a lesson, every delay a divine detour. The same hand that corrected me also carried me. What I once called coincidence, I now call providence. For the fear of the Lord has taught me that my life is not guided by luck or chance, but by divine design. The steps of the righteous are indeed ordered by the Lord, and grace—amazing grace—has been the bridge between my folly and my faith, between my wandering and my homecoming.

Meditative Reflection

The path of the upright is a journey of trust. Every turn is teaching, every valley preparation. The upright do not walk perfectly—they walk persistently. God's wisdom doesn't erase our humanity; it refines it. Breathe deeply and remember: the same grace that corrects your path also keeps your feet from falling.

Affirmation Prayer

El Elyon, Most High God,
Order my steps in Your Word.
Keep my heart steady in the way of righteousness.
Let wisdom guard me, and let Your Spirit preserve me.
Where I have strayed, lead me home again,
for Your counsel is my compass and Your grace my guide.
In the matchless Name of Yeshua, Amen.

Wisdom Key

Grace doesn't remove the path—it illuminates it.

Day 3
Trust in the Lord with All Your Heart

Proverbs 3:5–6

"Trust in the Lord with all thine heart; and lean not unto thine own understanding. In all thy ways acknowledge Him, and He shall direct thy paths."

Reflection
By Cheryl Walker, Lifetime Friend (LTF)

Cheryl Walker, my beloved Lifetime Friend of over fifty years, shares a testimony that beautifully embodies the sustaining power of divine trust. Her journey with Proverbs 3:5–6 began during one of life's heaviest storms—the painful separation from the father of her youngest son. With three children already depending on her strength, Cheryl found herself once again navigating the uncertain waters of single parenthood.

While attending a Bible study at her job at Drexel University, that timeless verse—"Trust in the Lord with all thine heart…"—pierced through her pain and found a permanent place in her spirit. Overwhelmed, she wept. But those tears became cleansing waters that washed away her burden. As she meditated and prayed, she felt the weight lift, replaced by the quiet assurance that God would guide her steps.

Years later, when love entered her life again, Cheryl wove Proverbs 3:5–6 into her wedding celebration—her cake shaped like an open Bible bearing those very words. Through the joys and trials of marriage, she leaned on that Scripture as her compass and her comfort.

Even after the passing of her beloved parents and other loved ones, Cheryl says she had "no other choice but to rely on that verse." In sleepless nights, in moments of anxiety, and in seasons of loss, Proverbs 3:5–6 became her refuge and her rhythm. When words fail, she prays that verse. When her children or family face hardship, she speaks it over them.

Today, Cheryl's testimony reminds us that Proverbs 3:5–6 isn't just a verse—it's a way of life. It's her "everyday, all-day, forever" Scripture. Through it all, her trust in the Lord has been her peace, her power, and her path home.

Meditative Reflection
Trust is not built in the absence of struggle—it is proven in it. When we can't trace His hand, we must trust His heart. Every unanswered prayer is still an invitation to believe that His direction is perfect, even when His pace feels slow.
Affirmation Prayer
Jehovah-Jireh, my Provider and Sustainer,
Teach me to trust You with all my heart.
When I cannot see, let faith be my vision.
When I cannot understand, let surrender be my strength.
Lead me in Your path, and let my life become a living testimony of trust.
In the matchless Name of Yeshua, Amen.

Wisdom Key
Trust turns waiting into worship.

Guard Your Heart with All Diligence

Proverbs 4:23
"Keep thy heart with all diligence; for out of it are
the issues of life."

Reflection

By Wanda B. Montague, Seer

This verse emphasizes that one's heart is the core of a person, and what fills it will ultimately shape their thoughts, words, and actions, determining the direction of their life. The heart is the source of all actions and life's "springs," meaning it's the wellspring of everything you do.

It is important to protect your heart with all diligence or vigilance because of its central importance. Guarding your heart involves being mindful of what you allow into your mind, as these thoughts will eventually affect your heart and, consequently, your life.

In this world today, I have found that in order to keep my heart and mind strengthened, I must focus on the things of God and His Kingdom above all else. In Him, I find my peace and my joy. In God, I am complete.

Meditative Reflection

Guarding the heart is more than protection—it is stewardship. Whatever we permit to enter eventually overflows. Keep watch over your heart as a sacred garden; what grows there will shape your entire life.

Affirmation Prayer

Jehovah-Shalom, my Peace and Protector,
Help me to guard my heart with diligence and delight.
Let nothing unworthy take root within me.
Fill me with peace, purify my desires, and make my heart Your
home.
In the matchless Name of Yeshua, Amen.

Wisdom Key

What you guard determines what you grow.

Wisdom Is the Principal Thing

Proverbs 4:7
"Wisdom is the principal thing; therefore get wisdom: and
with all thy getting get understanding."

Reflection

By Alnita Coulter, MNLP, MTT, HNt, MSC, and Trainer of
NLP

Knowledge is power. We have all heard this before. Applied
knowledge leads to understanding as we learn what works
and what doesn't. This consistent application eventually
creates the wisdom of knowing what works best in any given
situation. The knowledge gained from the application creates
additional insights that allow us to assess how effective a
particular solution will be, sometimes even before we engage
in the activity.

As long as I can remember, I have always had a passion for
knowledge. This is something I picked up from my father, Mr.
Oscar, as he was affectionately known. Boxes of unopened
books sat on our table since the shelves of our home's personal
library, which was made out of a converted coat closet,
were overflowing with books. As a child, I had an insatiable
curiosity to know why. I devoured books from our library and
eventually the school and public libraries on all topics from
Greek literature to the much lighter Amelia Bedelia books.

Some days, I would flip through the pages of our own personal
set of World Book Encyclopedias in search of exciting
things I could learn about. It wasn't enough to experience

something—I had to know more. This constant searching led to a more readily understanding of things that were going on around me. I wasn't just a participant. I was a keeper of knowledge related to how things worked or the richness of their history.

Sometimes I taught this information to imaginary classes. Other times, at just the right moment during a conversation, I would strategically share a tidbit of information on the subject—impressing them and satisfying me. Even if I gave a full discourse, I would smile because I knew there was always more to learn.

This thirst for knowledge has helped me lead a richer life. It provides insight into things I want to know more about and allows me to fill in the gaps of things I don't quite understand. While it's possible to lose things or even our way in life, it's impossible to lose the wisdom we gain from acquiring knowledge.

Once we learn something, even if we forget the details, it expands us and adds depth to our lives. Just like in a recipe, our knowledge and experiences are the things that add richness to our story. The more we learn, the more capable we become of creating something new—something meaningful.

Meditative Reflection

Wisdom is not the accumulation of facts—it's the transformation of understanding into grace. Knowledge informs, but wisdom reforms. It teaches us not just what is true, but how to live truthfully.

Pause and consider what wisdom has taught you through the trials that once felt like punishment. The lessons that last are those that sanctify the heart, not just stimulate the mind.

Affirmation Prayer

Elohim, Source of Infinite Understanding,
Open my mind to Your divine instruction.
Let every experience become a teacher and every challenge a classroom.
Grant me the humility to learn, the patience to apply, and the grace to grow.
Let wisdom crown my days and understanding guide my steps.
In the matchless Name of Yeshua, Amen.

Wisdom Key

Knowledge fills the mind; wisdom forms the soul.

Consider the Ant

Proverbs 6:6
"Go to the ant, thou sluggard; consider her ways,
and be wise."

Reflection

By Dr. Crystal Montague, Educator, Mother, and Grand-
mother

In Proverbs 6:6, we are advised to go to the ant—a small but
wise creature—for counsel. When we pause and consider the
ways of the ant, we see diligence, purpose, and preparation.
Though their lives are short, and only the queen lives for
many years, they work tirelessly to prepare for the future and
sustain generations to come.

In the same way, as believers, we may never meet Christ in
physical human form during our earthly lives, yet we continue
to labor in faith—nurturing our relationship with God while
setting an example for future generations to develop their own
deep and meaningful connection with the Almighty.

Unlike the sluggard, who lives only for the moment and
neglects opportunities to build upon their spirituality, we
should be inspired by the lesson of the ant and take it to
heart: to live with purpose, discipline, and faith. By doing so,
we draw nearer to God and learn to build a stronger, more
enduring relationship with Him.

Meditative Reflection

The ant's wisdom lies not in her strength, but in her strategy.

She teaches us that purpose is proven in preparation. Even when no one watches, she works—faithfully, quietly, efficiently. So it is with the faithful soul; consistency becomes a form of worship.

Affirmation Prayer

Jehovah-Tsidkenu, Lord Our Righteousness,
Inspire me to live diligently.
Help me to prepare today for the harvests of tomorrow.
May my labor be steady, my spirit steadfast, and my service sincere.
Let me build not for applause, but for legacy—
For Your glory and for those who follow behind me.
In the matchless Name of Yeshua, Amen.

Wisdom Key

Quiet diligence builds eternal legacy.

Day 7

The Pure Path

Proverbs 7:2
"Keep my commandments, and live;
and my law as the apple of thine eye."

Reflection

Purity is not perfection—it is alignment. It is the daily decision to walk in obedience rather than indulgence, in clarity rather than confusion. The pure path is not the easy one, but it is the protected one. It is the road where light and integrity meet.

The commandments of God are not chains—they are guardrails. They do not restrict life; they preserve it. When we keep His Word close, like the apple of our eye, we begin to see through divine lenses. His Word becomes the filter that clarifies motives, mends relationships, and corrects perception.

The world says to follow your heart; God says to guard it. The world says to chase your truth; God says to walk in His. The difference between the two is not subtle—it is eternal.

Meditative Reflection

The pure path begins in the secret place—where compromise dies and conviction lives. God's commandments are not burdens but blessings; they lead to freedom, not fear. The more we align with His Word, the more luminous our path becomes.

Pause for a moment. Ask the Lord to renew your desire for purity—not as performance, but as pursuit of presence.

Affirmation Prayer

Ruach HaKodesh, Holy Spirit,
Write Your law upon my heart.
Make my life a reflection of Your holiness.
When temptation whispers, let truth speak louder.
When confusion calls, let clarity answer.
Keep me on the pure path, and let obedience become my offering.
In the matchless Name of Yeshua, Amen.

Wisdom Key

Purity is not restraint—it is revelation. The clean heart sees clearly.

End of Week
Reflection

"The fear of the Lord is the beginning of wisdom: and the knowledge of the holy is understanding."

— Proverbs 9:10 (KJV)

Week One has brought us back to the beginning — not the beginning of information, but the beginning of orientation. Wisdom does not begin with answers; it begins with posture. It begins when the heart turns, the will bows, and the soul acknowledges that God is God, and we are not.

In these first seven days, we have learned that wisdom is not merely something to be acquired, but someone to be encountered. The fear of the Lord is not dread that repels us, but reverence that draws us near. It is the awakening realization that life is most secure, most meaningful, and most fruitful when lived in alignment with God's truth.

We have seen that wisdom calls us out of wandering and into intention. She invites us to guard our hearts, to trust the Lord beyond our own understanding, to value instruction, diligence, and obedience. She reminds us that grace redeems our missteps and that God patiently teaches those who are willing to learn.

This week has laid the foundation. Before wisdom builds anything lofty, she establishes what is solid. Before she reveals direction, she forms devotion. And before she grants understanding, she cultivates humility.

As we pause here, let us not rush ahead too quickly. Let us allow reverence to settle deeply into our spirits. For everything that follows — understanding, discernment, integrity, generosity, righteousness — will rise from this holy beginning.

Wisdom has opened the door.

The journey has begun.

Selah

WEEK TWO

"For the Lord giveth wisdom: out of his mouth cometh
knowledge and understanding."

— Proverbs 2:6 (KJV)

When wisdom calls, she does not shout above the noise.
She waits for stillness.
Her voice is the hush between thoughts,
the whisper beyond the world's constant demand to do.
She calls not to the hurried, but to the humble.
To those who will sit, listen, and yield.
Her instruction is not complicated—it is clear.
But clarity only comes to the heart at rest.
So pause here.
Breathe deeply.
Release the need to control, to fix, to force.
And in this quiet, let understanding rise like dawn over your
confusion.
For the Lord Himself gives wisdom,
and His words are light for every darkened path.

Selah.

Week Two

THE PATH OF UNDERSTANDING

Day 8

The Whisper Beyond the Noise

Proverbs 8:1
"Doth not wisdom cry? and understanding
put forth her voice?"

Reflection

Shush... do you hear it too?

That faint, haunting call—barely audible beyond the drone of duty, the rhythm of routine, the hum of habit. Somewhere in the static of everyday survival, someone is calling my name. Not with thunder, but with a whisper. Not demanding, but inviting.

And as I strain to listen, I realize—it's Wisdom herself. The same voice that walked through the streets of Solomon's

Jerusalem still wanders through the avenues of our hearts. She calls not from a distant temple but from within—the quiet chambers of conscience, the stillness between breaths.

Her tone is never frantic. She does not chase the hurried, but she waits for the humble. She is the voice that says, "Turn aside and live." And though the world rushes in a thousand directions, I find myself frozen in wonder. What does she require of me—and what do I require of her?

Perhaps this is where understanding begins—not in striving, but in stillness; not in noise, but in knowing. Wisdom speaks softly, but her words resound forever.

Meditative Reflection

Close your eyes.
Let the clamor fade until only the whisper remains.
In that stillness, she speaks—
not to inform, but to transform.

Affirmation Prayer

Ruach HaKodesh, Holy Spirit of Wisdom,
Tune my heart to Heaven's frequency.
Silence the static of worry and the noise of fear.
Teach me to hear Your whisper in the ordinary.
In the matchless Name of Yeshua, Amen.

Wisdom Key

Wisdom seldom shouts; she waits for the listener.

Day 9
The Fear of the Lord

Proverbs 9:10
"The fear of the Lord is the beginning of wisdom: and the knowledge of the holy is understanding."

Reflection by a Sister in Christ

To me, the fear of the Lord is not about dread—it is about divine reverence. It is to honor His presence, to yield to His voice, and to walk in obedience to His ways. True wisdom begins here—in humble awe before a Holy God.

When I think of Him, I remember Israel trembling at the mountain as the fire of His presence spoke. That trembling was not terror—it was the weight of glory pressing upon their souls. To stand before such holiness is to feel your humanity melt into worship.

The fear of the Lord brings order to chaos, clarity to confusion, and stability to the shifting sands of life. He is our Heavenly Father—good, loving, just. And like a good father, His correction is proof of His love. Every command is an anchor, every law a beam that holds up the house of wisdom.

To fear the Lord is to build wisely—to choose foundation over façade, obedience over opinion, and reverence over rebellion.

Meditative Reflection

Breathe in reverence.
Breathe out resistance.

Feel the steadiness that comes from surrender.
The fear of the Lord is not bondage—it is balance.

Affirmation Prayer

Jehovah-M'kaddesh, the Lord Who Sanctifies,
Teach me holy reverence.
Let awe replace arrogance.
Build my life upon the pillars of Your presence.
In the matchless Name of Yeshua, Amen.

Wisdom Key

Reverence is the root of stability; the heart that bows never breaks.

Integrity Is Quiet Strength

Proverbs 10:9
"He that walketh uprightly walketh surely: but he that perverteth his ways shall be known."

Reflection

Integrity is not performance—it is peace. It is the invisible companion that walks beside you when no one else sees. When you walk uprightly, you walk securely—not because the road is smooth, but because your footing is sure.

Enoch walked with God and did not taste death, for the Lord took him. That single line stirs something deep in me. Walking with God is not about pace or perfection—it's about direction and devotion. Each morning, I choose to walk upright, consciously and deliberately, aligning my steps with His will.

I have known duplicity—the anxiety of divided living, the fear of exposure. But integrity picked me up, brushed off the dust, and whispered, "Keep walking." Even when unseen, integrity shines before Heaven's eyes.

Let it be said of us: we walked uprightly before our God. For integrity doesn't keep us from falling—it keeps us from staying down.

Meditative Reflection

Take one step at a time.
Let truth lead, not fear.
Integrity is the narrow road that leads to broad peace.

Affirmation Prayer

Jehovah-Tsidkenu, my Righteousness,
Establish my walk in Your truth.
Let my words and ways align.
Anchor me in honesty and clothe me in grace.
In the matchless Name of Yeshua, Amen.

Wisdom Key

Integrity is the armor of the soul; it silences every accusation.

Words That Build, Not Break

Proverbs 11:11
"By the blessing of the upright the city is exalted: but it is
overthrown by the mouth of the wicked."

Reflection

Every word is a seed—either of blessing or of blight. Cities rise
or fall, hearts heal or harden, destinies flourish or fade—all by
the power of the tongue.

When I learned to bless more than I complained, my
atmosphere shifted. When I spoke life instead of loss, peace
began to govern my day. God entrusted us with creative
language: the same Spirit that hovered over chaos now hovers
over every spoken word.

The upright do not use their mouths to curse their cities, their
families, or themselves. They build, encourage, and uplift.
Blessing is not denial of reality—it is declaration of divine
possibility.

Meditative Reflection

Pause before you speak.
Is this word planting life or poisoning ground?
Let your mouth become a sanctuary where only praise resides.

Affirmation Prayer

Jehovah-Rapha, the Lord Who Heals,
Heal my heart that my words may heal others.

Let blessing overflow from my lips as worship.
Teach me to speak life into every barren place.
In the matchless Name of Yeshua, Amen.

Wisdom Key

When you bless with your mouth, you build with your life.

Day 12
The Law of Return

Proverbs 12:14
"From the fruit of their lips people are filled with good things,
and the work of their hands brings them reward."

Reflection

Life moves in divine cycles. What we release eventually returns. Every act, every word, every seed—spiritual, emotional, or financial—sets something in motion that circles back, pressed down, shaken together, and running over.

Paul declared, "Be not deceived; God is not mocked. For whatsoever a man soweth, that shall he also reap." And Jesus confirmed, "Give, and it shall be given unto you." The old African American Nana was right: "You can't out-give God."

When we open our hands, hearts, and mouths in generosity, Heaven opens in response. Every seed carries resurrection potential. Blessings don't vanish—they circulate.

So today, guard your words, guide your works, and give with an open spirit. Every good seed will find its season of return.

Meditative Reflection

See your words as wings.
They travel far, but they always return.
Sow peace. Sow kindness. Sow praise.

Affirmation Prayer

El Shaddai, All-Sufficient One,
Teach me to sow with joy and to give with faith.
Make me a channel of blessing, not a reservoir of fear.
Let my harvest bring glory to Your Name.
In the matchless Name of Yeshua, Amen.

Wisdom Key

Whatever you release in faith will always find its way back multiplied.

Day 13

Hope Restored

Proverbs 13:12
"Hope deferred maketh the heart sick: but when the desire
cometh, it is a tree of life."

Reflection

Heaven has heard the cry of waiting souls—those white-robed
saints beneath the altar who cried, "How long, O Lord, how
long?" Their voices echo the ache of every believer who has
prayed, waited, believed, and yet not seen.

Hope deferred can make the heart faint. But waiting is not
wasted. In waiting, faith is refined, patience perfected, and the
soul roots deeper in divine trust. The silence of Heaven is not
God's absence—it's His sacred invitation to rest in His timing.

When God finally answers, He does not merely respond with
words but with revelation—"after a while, and a little while
longer." That phrase carries eternal fragrance: though the
vision tarries, wait for it—it shall surely come.

Every deferred dream, every tear sown in faith, will blossom
into joy unspeakable and full of glory.

Meditative Reflection

Hope is not lost—it is resting.
In the quiet soil of faith, unseen promises grow.
Wait well. God has not forgotten.

Affirmation Prayer

Jehovah-Jireh, my Provider of Promise,
Renew my strength in the waiting.
Turn delay into discipline and silence into song.
Fulfill every longing according to Your perfect time.
In the matchless Name of Yeshua, Amen.

Wisdom Key

Waiting seasons are not empty—they are wombs where miracles form.

Day 14

Wisdom Builds the House

Proverbs 14:1

"Every wise woman buildeth her house: but the foolish
plucketh it down with her hands."

Reflection

Wisdom is a builder; folly is a breaker. Every decision lays a
brick—either in the wall of peace or the rubble of regret. The
wise do not build overnight; they build over time.

Whether it's a home, a marriage, a ministry, or a mind—
building takes patience, prayer, and perseverance. Wisdom
does not shout; she measures. She discerns which words heal,
which wounds need tending, which walls must stand, and
which must come down.

The foolish tear with emotion; the wise build with devotion.
Wisdom's foundation is understanding, her mortar is love,
and her roof is grace.

Meditative Reflection

What are you building with your words today?
With your choices? With your silence?
The home of your heart is built one decision at a time.

Affirmation Prayer

El Olam, Everlasting God,
Make me a wise builder of every space You entrust to me.

Let my love restore what life has broken.
Build my heart into a dwelling of Your peace.
In the matchless Name of Yeshua, Amen.

Wisdom Key

The house wisdom builds will always outlast the storm.

End of Week
Reflection

"Wisdom is the principal thing; therefore get wisdom: and with all thy getting get understanding."
Proverbs 4:7 (KJV)

This week has taught us that wisdom is not a destination we arrive at, but a path we learn to walk—slowly, reverently, and with intention. Understanding does not rush ahead of us; it unfolds as we yield. It meets us in quiet obedience, in careful words, in upright steps, and in patient waiting.

We have learned that wisdom whispers where pride would shout. She anchors herself in the fear of the Lord—not fear that paralyzes, but reverence that steadies. From that holy ground, integrity becomes our companion, our words become builders, and our choices become seeds sown into tomorrow.

Understanding has shown us that life is deeply responsive. What we speak returns. What we sow multiplies. What we build endures. Even hope deferred, painful as it is, has not been wasted—because God is still working beneath the surface, shaping hearts strong enough to steward fulfilled promises.

By the end of this week, we realize that wisdom is not merely about knowing what is right, but about becoming aligned with what is true. It builds houses, restores hope, and trains the soul to trust God's timing more than its own urgency.

So we pause here—not to stop the journey, but to honor the progress.

We breathe. We listen.

We acknowledge the quiet work God has done within us.

May the understanding gained this week become a foundation for the days ahead.

May wisdom continue to shape our thoughts, govern our words, and guide our steps.

And may the Lord, who gives wisdom freely, continue to light our path—one faithful step at a time.

Selah

WEEK THREE

"Trust in the Lord with all thine heart; and lean not unto
thine own understanding."
— Proverbs 3:5 (KJV)

Faith does not need proof to stand — only trust to lean.

The heart that trusts God learns to breathe even when life
trembles.

It releases the need to control outcomes and rests instead in
the wisdom of divine timing.

Trust is not passive; it is the quiet courage to believe when
sight fails.

It is the bridge between promise and fulfillment,

the sacred stillness between "not yet" and "now."

When the winds rise and the path feels uncertain,

trust becomes your shelter.

When the waiting grows long and the answers seem delayed,

trust becomes your prayer.

This week, let faith sink deeper than fear.

Let your soul learn to rest, not in the rhythm of results,

but in the heartbeat of the One who holds all things together.

Selah

THE HEART OF TRUST

Day 15
The Power of Words

Proverbs 18:21

"Death and life are in the power of the tongue: and they that love it shall eat the fruit thereof."

Reflection

I have learned that words do not vanish — they vibrate through eternity. They are sound wrapped in spirit, carrying life or death in every syllable. God spoke, and light leapt from nothing. Jesus spoke, and the dead breathed again. Every believer holds that same sacred authority in their mouth — a creative power that shapes realities, frames destinies, and establishes atmospheres.

There was a season when my speech betrayed my faith. I prayed for breakthroughs, but my words built barriers. I declared hope while confessing defeat. Then the Spirit reminded me: "You cannot walk in what you will not speak." My tongue was steering my soul off course.

When I began blessing instead of complaining, life began to align. Peace settled where panic had lived. Healing flowed where bitterness had festered. God showed me that the tongue is a rudder — small, but mighty. It turns ships and souls alike.

Every word is a seed. Speak faith, and fruit will follow. Speak fear, and weeds will grow. Your life today is the harvest of yesterday's confession. Choose your words as carefully as you would choose the seed for your field. For whatever you plant, you will surely eat.

Meditative Reflection

Pause and place a hand over your lips.
Whisper: "My mouth is a vessel of light."
Breathe deeply and remember — words are not mere sounds.
They are instruments of spirit, shaping the world you live in.

Affirmation Prayer

Ruach HaKodesh, Spirit of the Living God,
Sanctify my lips and anoint my words.
Let truth drip like honey from my tongue.
Teach me to speak life into lifeless places.
Make my speech a song of faith that Heaven recognizes.
In the matchless Name of Yeshua, Amen.

Wisdom Key

What you speak today becomes the soil of your tomorrow.

Day 16
Commit Your Plans to the Lord

Proverbs 16:3

"Commit thy works unto the Lord, and thy thoughts
shall be established."

Reflection

Every dream I've ever dared to hold began as a whisper
from God — and every time I tried to build it on my own,
it collapsed under the weight of my control. There is a peace
that only comes when we surrender our blueprints to Heaven.

To commit our works to the Lord is to lay them down on the
altar of trust. It means acknowledging that God knows where
we're going, even when we do not. His plans do not need our
permission; they need our participation. When we yield, He
leads.

There was a time when I prayed, "Lord, bless my plans." Now
I pray, "Lord, let Your plans bless me." When I stopped trying
to convince God to follow my strategy, He started revealing
His sovereignty.

Commitment births clarity. What we surrender, God
strengthens. The steps of a good man are ordered by the Lord
— and when those steps feel slow or uncertain, it is often
because grace is adjusting the pace to match His will.

So, let every ambition become an offering. Every goal a gift
back to the Giver. When your works are committed, your
thoughts become established — because your mind is resting
in His peace.

Meditative Reflection

Hold your plans in open hands.
Say softly: "Lord, not my will, but Yours."
See your plans rising like incense, carried by trust.
Release the need to know. Rest in the joy of being led.

Affirmation Prayer

El Elyon, Most High God,

I place every plan beneath Your authority.

Make my ambitions holy and my actions fruitful.

Establish my thoughts in peace and align my path with purpose.

In the matchless Name of Yeshua, Amen.

Wisdom Key

God can only direct what you're willing to release.

Day 17

A Friend Loves at All Times

Proverbs 17:17

"A friend loveth at all times, and a brother is born
for adversity."

Reflection

True friendship is a ministry of presence. It's love that stays
when explanations fail, compassion that covers when life
exposes. The kind of friend who stands beside you in adversity
is not an accident — they are a divine assignment.

I've walked through valleys where fair-weather companions
disappeared like mist, but the God-sent ones stayed. They
didn't offer clichés or quick fixes; they offered prayer, patience,
and presence. Those friends reflected the heart of Jesus — the
One who called us "friends," not servants, because He was
willing to bear our burdens.

Love at all times means love without conditions. It's
faithfulness that doesn't fluctuate with seasons. It's loyalty that
doesn't look for reward. Adversity reveals authenticity. When
the storm clears, you'll know who your brothers truly are

If you have even one such friend, treasure them. If you are that
friend to someone, know that Heaven sees your consistency as
worship. For a friend who loves like Christ is a mirror of His
mercy in motion.

Meditative Reflection

Think of a friend who stood by you in the dark.
Whisper their name in gratitude.
Now think of one who needs your presence today.
Resolve to be that reflection of God's faithfulness.

Affirmation Prayer

Jehovah-Raah, my Shepherd and Friend,
Thank You for covenant companions.
Teach me to love without limits, to give without counting.
Let my loyalty become a living testimony of Your heart.
In the matchless Name of Yeshua, Amen.

Wisdom Key

True friends don't just stand with you — they stand for you.

Day 18
The Name of the Lord Is a Strong Tower

Proverbs 18:10
"The name of the Lord is a strong tower: the righteous run-
neth into it, and is safe."

Reflection

There are days when fear knocks louder than faith. When the
storm rages and reason fails, there is one place I know I can
run — the Name of the Lord.

That Name is not mere syllables; it is substance. When I
whisper "Jehovah," strength fills the air around me. When I
breathe "Yeshua," peace floods the corridors of my soul. The
Name of the Lord is not a label — it is a fortress made of Spirit,
a sanctuary built by eternity itself.

I have run into that Name many times — in grief, in danger, in
confusion. Each time, the tower stood immovable. The walls
of His faithfulness surrounded me. The gates of His mercy
opened to receive me. I realized that safety is not absence of
battle; it is presence within the Builder.

When the righteous run into that Name, they are not escaping
the world — they are entering divine defense. His Name is a
place. His Name is power. His Name is peace.

Meditative Reflection

Close your eyes and whisper His Name.
Let "Yeshua" become your breath prayer.

Every repetition is a step into safety.
You are enclosed, beloved, secure.

Affirmation Prayer

Jehovah-Nissi, my Banner and Defender,
You are my strong tower.
I run into Your Name and find rest.
Be my fortress when I am weary, my peace when I am afraid.
Let Your Name be my home forever.
In the matchless Name of Yeshua, Amen.

Wisdom Key

The Name of the Lord is not just spoken — it's entered.

Day 19
The Power of Patience

Proverbs 19:11
"The discretion of a man deferreth his anger; and it is his glory to pass over a transgression."

Reflection

Patience is the art of divine timing. It's not the absence of feeling — it's the mastery of reaction. Every delay that tests your patience is training your discretion.

I've learned that anger burns fast but fades quickly; patience burns slow but refines deeply. To hold your peace when provoked is not weakness — it's wisdom wrapped in restraint. God Himself is patient beyond measure. He waits on nations, nurtures generations, and redeems the rebellious with grace.

When we reflect His patience, we manifest His glory. Passing over offense doesn't mean pretending it didn't hurt — it means refusing to hand your peace over to pain. The higher your calling, the greater your calm must be.

Patience doesn't always change your circumstance, but it will always change you.

Meditative Reflection

Breathe in peace, breathe out pride.
The anger you withhold today becomes the grace you'll need tomorrow.
Let patience have her perfect work.

Affirmation Prayer

Jehovah-Shalom, my Prince of Peace,
Still my storms within and without.
Teach me to wait well and to respond with grace.
Crown me with calm and clothe me with understanding.
In the matchless Name of Yeshua, Amen.

Wisdom Key

Patience is wisdom in motion.

Day 20

The Glory of a King Is to Overlook a Matter

Proverbs 20:3
"It is an honour for a man to cease from strife:
but every fool will be meddling."

Reflection

It takes greater strength to walk away than to win an argument.

The world confuses noise with power, but Heaven honors silence born of peace.

Kings are not drawn into petty battles. They know that energy wasted on offense is energy stolen from purpose. When you choose peace, you protect your crown. The fool must always have the last word; the wise know the value of restraint.

There was a time when I answered every provocation. Every false word about me demanded a rebuttal — until God whispered, "Let Me defend you." And He did. The battle I stopped fighting became the testimony I started living.

Peace is not passive — it's powerful. When you cease from strife, you do not lose face; you reveal maturity. The glory of a king is calm in conflict, silence in accusation, grace under pressure.

Meditative Reflection

Picture your crown — peace polished by patience.
Now imagine your hands too full of offense to hold it.
Let go. Step back. Choose stillness.

Affirmation Prayer

El Gibbor, Mighty God,
Grant me royal restraint.
Help me to rise above the pettiness that steals peace.
Let my silence speak louder than my defense.
Crown me with wisdom that walks in calmness.
In the matchless Name of Yeshua, Amen.

Wisdom Key

Sometimes victory is walking away still dignified.

Day 21

The Righteous Are Bold as a Lion

Proverbs 28:1
"The wicked flee when no man pursueth: but the righteous
are bold as a lion."

Reflection

Fear used to follow me like a shadow — fear of failing, fear of falling short, fear of being seen and still not being enough. But righteousness changed my posture. When I finally understood that I was accepted by God, not because of my perfection but because of His, courage came alive in me.

The wicked run from shadows; the righteous run toward destiny. The lion does not apologize for its roar, and neither should the redeemed. Your roar is your witness — the sound of your testimony echoing against fear.

Righteousness gives you authority. It anchors your confidence not in ability, but in identity. You are blood-bought, Spirit-filled, Heaven-sent. You are not timid; you are trusted.

When you walk in that truth, you no longer shrink. You stride. Boldness is not rebellion — it's revelation. It's living from the inside out, unashamed of the One who called you by name.

Meditative Reflection

Lift your head high.
You are the righteousness of God in Christ Jesus.
Your boldness is not arrogance — it's alignment.
Walk as a lion among lambs — gentle, yet unafraid.

Affirmation Prayer

El Gibbor, Mighty Warrior,
Roar through me when I feel small.
Fill me with the confidence of Heaven.
Let my courage become contagious.
Help me to live boldly, love deeply, and stand firmly in faith.
In the matchless Name of Yeshua, Amen.

Wisdom Key

Boldness is not in your volume — it's in your virtue.

End of Week
Reflection

This week has drawn us into the holy discipline of trust—not as an idea to admire, but as a posture to inhabit. We have learned that trust is not forged in certainty, but in surrender. It is the courage to lean when understanding runs out, to rest when answers delay, and to believe when circumstances resist explanation.

We discovered that trust shapes our speech. Words spoken in faith become seeds of life; words spoken in fear become architects of limitation. The tongue revealed itself as both compass and rudder—guiding the direction of the soul. As we committed our plans to the Lord, we learned that clarity follows surrender, and peace attends obedience.

Trust also revealed itself through people—friends who love without condition, brothers and sisters born for adversity. Through them, God reminds us that we were never meant to walk this journey alone. And when the storms rose, we learned where to run—not away from the battle, but into the Name that stands as an unshakable tower.

Patience taught us restraint. Peace taught us dignity. We learned that wisdom sometimes speaks by saying nothing at all, and that honor is often found in walking away whole rather than winning a momentary argument. In that stillness, trust matured into strength.

By the close of this week, trust gave birth to boldness. Not the loud confidence of pride, but the quiet courage of righteousness. The kind of boldness that does not flee shadows, because it walks in light. The righteous do not run because they know who stands with them—and who stands within them.

So we pause again.

Not because the journey is complete,

but because trust has deepened.

May what we have learned this week teach us to lean more fully,

to speak more faithfully,

to walk more patiently,

and to stand more boldly.

For the heart that trusts the Lord does not collapse under pressure—

it rests securely in the One who holds all things together.

Selah

WEEK FOUR

"Her ways are ways of pleasantness, and
all her paths are peace."
— Proverbs 3:17 (KJV)

Wisdom walks softly.
She does not shout to be heard,
nor rush to be followed.
She invites the humble, the listening, the teachable —
those whose hearts have been softened by trust
and whose ears have been trained by obedience.
Her path is narrow, but it is pleasant.
Her steps are steady, but they lead to peace.
She guides the soul that has grown weary of striving,
and whispers, "There is another way — My way."
The Way of Wisdom is not paved with perfection,
but with discernment.
It is not traveled by the proud,
but by the patient.
Along her road are signposts of grace,
fountains of understanding,
and crossroads where the Spirit still speaks.
If you listen, you can hear her calling even now —
inviting you to walk more gently,
to think more deeply,
to love more purely.
This week, let us journey the Way of Wisdom.
Let us trade anxiety for alignment,
haste for holiness,
and pride for peace.
For all her paths are peace —
and peace is the proof that you are walking with God.

Selah

THE WAY OF WISDOM

Day 22

A Good Name Is Rather to Be Chosen Than Great Riches

Proverbs 22:1
"A good name is rather to be chosen than great riches, and
loving favour rather than silver and gold."

Reflection

Names have weight. They carry echoes of who we are and what we've stood for. Some are whispered with affection; others are spoken with caution. Your name travels into rooms you've never entered and lingers long after you've left.

In my youth, I admired those who chased wealth. I believed prosperity was proof of success. But as I matured in faith, I learned that riches can be lost in a night — while a good name endures for generations.

A good name isn't built on charm or charisma, but on consistency. It's forged in the fires of adversity and sealed by the choices we make when no one is watching. Integrity is the currency of Heaven — and it's worth more than gold.

When God establishes your name, no slander can destroy it. When His favor rests on you, your reputation becomes His reflection. Better to be known as faithful than famous, as honest than affluent.

Because one day, when history fades and all titles fall silent, it will not be your wealth that speaks for you — it will be your name.

Meditative Reflection

Close your eyes.
Say your own name softly.
Ask God to make it a fragrance of righteousness,
a melody Heaven recognizes,
a story worth remembering.

Affirmation Prayer

Jehovah-Tsidkenu, Lord My Righteousness,
Sanctify my name.
Let my integrity shine brighter than success.
Guard my reputation as I walk before You in truth.
Let favor follow faithfulness, and honor follow humility.
In the matchless Name of Yeshua, Amen.

Wisdom Key

A good name is a treasure Heaven deposits in the hearts of men.

Day 23
Humility Comes Before Honor

Proverbs 22:4
"By humility and the fear of the Lord are riches,
and honour, and life."

Reflection

Humility is Heaven's doorway — the threshold every soul must cross to find true greatness. Pride builds towers that crumble; humility lays foundations that last.

There was a time when I mistook humility for weakness. I thought strength meant being seen, being right, being first. But humility is not silence — it is surrender. It is the quiet courage to kneel before God while others race for thrones.

When you humble yourself, you make room for God's glory to rise. Scripture doesn't say that humility leads to humiliation; it says it leads to riches, honor, and life. That is divine irony — those who bow lowest are lifted highest.

Jesus Himself modeled it perfectly. Though He was equal with God, He took the form of a servant — and because He humbled Himself, God exalted His Name above every name.

The path to promotion is paved with humility. When you walk low, Heaven looks high upon you.

Meditative Reflection

Breathe out pride.
Breathe in peace.

See humility not as a lowering,
but as an alignment — a returning to grace.

Affirmation Prayer

El Elyon, Most High God,
Keep me small in my own eyes and great in Yours.
Let humility be the fragrance of my soul.
Exalt me only to the degree that I exalt You.
In the matchless Name of Yeshua, Amen.

Wisdom Key

Heaven always exalts the one who kneels first.

Day 24
The Rich and the Poor Meet Together

Proverbs 22:2
"The rich and poor meet together: the Lord is the maker of them all."

Reflection

The marketplace of life has many voices — some loud with power, others hushed with struggle. Yet when Heaven looks upon humanity, there are no classes — only creations.

God is no respecter of persons. The rich and the poor breathe the same air, share the same mortality, and are measured by the same mercy. Wealth does not make one favored, nor does poverty make one forgotten. Both stand level before the Lord who made them.

Wisdom teaches compassion over comparison. The hand that gives and the hand that receives were shaped by the same Potter. When we see through Heaven's eyes, we stop measuring worth by wallets and begin valuing souls by their divine design.

You may be the one who gives today — but tomorrow you may be the one who needs grace. Life humbles us all. The true wealth of wisdom is learning to see God's image in everyone you meet.

Meditative Reflection

When you encounter another soul today,

pause and silently whisper, "Made by God."
It will change how you see them —
and how you treat them.

Affirmation Prayer

Jehovah-Raah, my Shepherd,
Open my eyes to the divine in every person.
Remove pride from my vision and prejudice from my heart.
Let love level every boundary until compassion becomes my
wealth.
In the matchless Name of Yeshua, Amen.

Wisdom Key

Every face bears the fingerprints of God.

Day 25
He That Hath a Bountiful Eye
Shall Be Blessed

Proverbs 22:9
"He that hath a bountiful eye shall be blessed; for he giveth of his bread to the poor."

Reflection

A bountiful eye is not just generous — it is perceptive. It sees beyond lack to potential, beyond need to opportunity. It recognizes that blessing is not possession, but participation in the heart of God.

Generosity is not measured by the size of the gift, but by the spirit behind it. The one who gives freely declares, "God is my Source." The open hand never empties; it becomes a conduit for Heaven's flow.

I once watched a woman at a food pantry offer her last two cans of soup to a stranger with more need than she. She smiled and said, "It's just soup — but it's love too." That moment preached a sermon without words.

The bountiful eye is the eye of Christ. It looks upon the hungry, the weary, the forgotten, and says, "You are seen." When you give what you have, God multiplies what remains.

Meditative Reflection

Look for someone to bless today.
Not because you must, but because you can.
The heart that gives in secret is never empty in spirit.

Affirmation Prayer

El Shaddai, All-Sufficient One,
Make my eyes generous and my hands open.
Teach me to give as You give — joyfully, freely, abundantly.
Let generosity become my worship and compassion my legacy.
In the matchless Name of Yeshua, Amen!

Wisdom Key

When you open your hand to give, Heaven opens its hand to bless.

As a Man Thinketh in His Heart, So Is He

Proverbs 23:7
"For as he thinketh in his heart, so is he."

Reflection

Your mind is a garden, and your thoughts are the seeds. Whatever you plant there, you will eventually live among.

I once lived bound by the weeds of negative thinking. I prayed for joy, but meditated on fear. I confessed faith, but rehearsed failure. The Spirit convicted me gently: "You cannot think one way and live another." My outer life was mirroring my inner meditation.

When I renewed my mind with the Word, my world began to change. Peace replaced panic. Vision returned where doubt had lived. I realized that thoughts create atmosphere — and atmospheres invite outcomes.

To think like Heaven is to align your mind with truth. Scripture is not just to be read — it is to be rewired into the way you see yourself.

Think on what is pure, lovely, and of good report. Think like the redeemed. Think like the healed. Think like the loved. For as a man thinketh in his heart, so is he.

Meditative Reflection

Place your hand on your heart and whisper, "Lord, renew my mind."

Imagine His Word washing your thoughts clean.
Today, think like grace is real — because it is.

Affirmation Prayer

El Roi, God Who Sees Me,
Transform my thoughts with truth.
Let my mind mirror Your wisdom and my heart hold Your peace.
Silence every voice that contradicts Your Word.
In the matchless Name of Yeshua, Amen.

Wisdom Key

Your thoughts are architects; build something worth living in.

Day 27
As Iron Sharpens Iron

Proverbs 27:17
"Iron sharpeneth iron; so a man sharpeneth the countenance of his friend."

Reflection

Growth happens in friction. Sparks fly when iron meets iron — but that's how the blade becomes sharp.

Relationships that refine you are gifts from God. The people who challenge you are not your enemies; they are Heaven's instruments, chiseling you into shape. Every rebuke wrapped in love, every confrontation born of truth, is part of your sharpening.

Some friendships exist only for comfort, but divine connections exist for growth. They will not always agree with you — but they will always call you higher.

Cherish those who speak truth, even when it stings. The wounds of a friend are faithful because they heal deeper than the flattery of foes. Wisdom doesn't isolate; it invests.

Meditative Reflection

Think of someone who has sharpened you — through honesty, through love, through challenge.
Whisper a prayer of gratitude.
Ask God to make you that kind of friend in someone else's life.

Affirmation Prayer

El Gibbor, Mighty God,
Thank You for those who refine me through truth.
Give me humility to receive correction and courage to offer it
in love.
Let every friendship forge my faith and strengthen my purpose.
In the matchless Name of Yeshua, Amen.

Wisdom Key

The friends who challenge you today are sharpening you for
tomorrow.

Where There Is No Vision, the People Perish

Proverbs 29:18
"Where there is no vision, the people perish: but he that keepeth the law, happy is he."

Reflection

Vision is the oxygen of the soul. Without it, life suffocates under routine. Vision gives direction to discipline and meaning to motion.

When God gives you a vision, He is entrusting you with a fragment of His eternal plan. But every vision demands obedience. Dreams without discipline are distractions.

There was a time when I saw glimpses of purpose but lacked the patience to wait for process. I mistook inspiration for readiness. Vision is not just seeing — it's staying. Staying faithful when the dream is distant, staying obedient when the outcome is unclear.

To keep the vision alive, you must keep the Word alive in you. The law sustains the light. The Scriptures sharpen the sight. The heart that obeys what it already knows will be trusted with more revelation.

Vision is not lost — it's often waiting on obedience.

Meditative Reflection

What has God shown you that you've stopped pursuing? Revisit it in prayer.

Ask Him to rekindle what routine has dimmed.
The dream still breathes — it's just waiting for your faith to inhale again.

Affirmation Prayer

Jehovah-Rohi, my Shepherd and Guide,
Open my eyes to see Your hand in my journey.
Restore vision where doubt has dimmed it.
Let obedience become my worship and faith my lens.
In the matchless Name of Yeshua, Amen.

Wisdom Key

Vision fades where obedience fails, but flourishes where faith endures.

"I have taught thee in the way of wisdom; I have led thee in right paths. When thou goest, thy steps shall not be straitened; and when thou runnest, thou shalt not stumble."

Proverbs 4:11-12

This week has reminded us that wisdom is not merely something we learn—it is a way we walk. Not hurried, not harsh, not driven by comparison or ambition, but guided gently by discernment, humility, and peace. The Way of Wisdom does not promise ease, but it always produces rest.

We have learned that wisdom shapes our reputation before it ever increases our resources. A good name, forged through integrity and faithfulness, outlives wealth and speaks long after possessions fade. We discovered that humility is not self-erasure, but divine alignment—the posture that invites honor without demanding it.

Wisdom also trained our eyes. It taught us to see every person as God's creation, every need as an opportunity for compassion, and every act of generosity as an echo of Heaven's heart. Along this path, we learned that abundance flows not from what we accumulate, but from what we are willing to give.

Our thoughts, too, were brought under wisdom's care. We saw that the inner life governs the outer journey, and that peace begins where truth reshapes the mind. We learned that growth is often sharpened through relationships—through honest friends who love us enough to refine us—and that vision, when guarded by obedience, keeps the soul alive and directed.

By the close of this week, one truth stands clear: wisdom's way leads somewhere. It leads away from striving and toward stability. Away from noise and toward clarity. Away from pride and toward peace.

So we pause again—mid-journey, but well-guided.

We slow our steps.

We steady our hearts.

We give thanks for a path that does not exhaust, but restores.

May the Way of Wisdom continue to order our thoughts, temper our words, shape our relationships, and clarify our vision. And may the peace that marks her paths become the quiet confirmation that we are walking with God.

Selah

WEEK FIVE

"The path of the righteous is as the shining light, that shineth
more and more unto the perfect day."
— Proverbs 4:18 (KJV)

There is a brightness that no darkness can dim —
the steady glow of a life aligned with God.
The righteous do not burn out; they burn on,
because their fire is not fueled by fame or fortune,
but by faith.
Righteousness is not perfection —
it is pursuit.
It is walking in the light even when the road is narrow,
and choosing obedience when compromise seems easier.
The path of righteousness does not promise ease,
but it guarantees clarity.
Each step reveals more of God's heart,
and with every act of obedience, the light grows stronger.
Those who walk this path discover hidden treasures:
peace that cannot be purchased,
joy that does not depend on circumstance,
and favor that follows like sunlight through the trees.
This week, we celebrate the fruit of faithfulness.
Every tear, every test, every turning point has led you here —
to the radiant reward of walking rightly before God.
So lift your head, beloved.
Your journey is not in vain.
The light that guides you is growing brighter.
Keep walking,
for your next step will only shine more.

Selah

THE REWARDS OF RIGHTEOUSNESS

Day 29

The Righteous Are Bold as a Lion

Proverbs 28:1
"The wicked flee when no man pursueth:
but the righteous are bold as a lion."

Reflection

There was a time when fear held me hostage — fear of failure, fear of rejection, fear of being seen and still not being chosen. But righteousness — true righteousness — broke those chains.

The moment I understood that righteousness was not earned, but imparted through Christ, courage was born in me. It was no longer about being flawless; it was about being forgiven. The wicked flee from shadows because they know they are unprotected. But the righteous — clothed in Christ's light — stand fearless, because they know they are covered.

Boldness is not arrogance; it is awareness. It is the steady confidence that comes from knowing who you are and whose you are. The lion does not announce itself to the jungle — it simply roars, and the atmosphere adjusts.

The righteous roar too — not in pride, but in purpose. Their words carry authority because their hearts carry purity. The boldness of the righteous is not found in their volume, but in their virtue. They move in power because Heaven moves with them.

So today, walk in that boldness. Speak truth with courage. Love with conviction. Pray with power. You are not called to cower — you are called to conquer.

Meditative Reflection

Breathe deeply.
Feel your heartbeat align with Heaven's rhythm.
Whisper, "I am the righteousness of God in Christ Jesus."
Let the truth settle — you are bold because you are beloved.

Affirmation Prayer

El Gibbor, Mighty God,
Make me bold in faith and fearless in purpose.
Silence the voice of fear within me and amplify the sound of courage.
Let my life roar with righteousness,
and may every step I take declare that I belong to You.
In the matchless Name of Yeshua, Amen.

Wisdom Key

Boldness is not rebellion — it's revelation of who you are in Him.

Day 30
The Just Man Walks in His Integrity

Proverbs 20:7
"The just man walketh in his integrity: his children are
blessed after him."

Reflection

Integrity is the invisible inheritance we leave to those who
follow us. It's not what we say that shapes them most — it's
how we live when no one is watching.

A just man walks in integrity, not because it's easy, but because
it's eternal. His compass is not culture — it is character. His
reward is not applause — it is peace.

Integrity means wholeness — being the same in private as you
are in public, the same in your thoughts as in your testimony.
The one who walks in integrity walks securely because truth
has no need to hide.

Our children and spiritual heirs do not just inherit our words;
they inherit our ways. When they see consistency, they learn
conviction. When they see honesty, they learn honor. Integrity
plants seeds of blessing that grow long after we are gone.

There will always be shortcuts that promise success without
sacrifice — but they come at the cost of legacy. Walk uprightly.
Let your life be a sermon your children will never forget.

Meditative Reflection

Visualize your footsteps — each one leaving a mark on soft
soil.

Behind you walk those you love.

Pray, "Lord, let my steps be steady, my path be pure, and my integrity leave a trail of blessing."

Affirmation Prayer

Jehovah-Tsidkenu, Lord My Righteousness,
Keep my heart whole before You.
Let integrity be my inheritance and truth my testimony.
May those who come after me find a faithful path beneath their feet.
In the matchless Name of Yeshua, Amen.

Wisdom Key

Integrity is not taught by words — it's transferred by example.

The Faithful and Virtuous Woman

Proverbs 31:10
"A wife of noble character who can find? She is worth far
more than rubies."

Reflection
by Dr. Zanessa Murphy, D.D. — Philadelphia, PA

What does it mean to be faithful? What does noble character
look like?

He had broken her heart and assassinated her character. He
had struck her mother to the floor and taken money out of
their home to feed a habit she had already survived once
before. Yet, at 3 A.M., the phone rang — it was him. His voice
trembled: "Ness, I'm hungry. I'm cold… I don't know what to
do."

She walked quietly to the kitchen, searching cupboards
and refrigerator for anything she could prepare quickly —
something to meet his need. She filled a bag with food and
stood there for a moment, tears forming as her best friend
exclaimed, "I know you're not taking him any food! After
everything he did to you? How can you even think about
helping him?"

Another tear slipped down her face as she softly replied,

"Because… I was him."

Faithfulness is not simply a word — it is a posture of the heart.
It's love that remains when reason has run out. It is the quiet

endurance that does good even when goodness has not been returned.

To be faithful is to reflect the very heart of God — steadfast, compassionate, unchanging. Faithfulness is the glue that holds virtue together; it's divine endurance that says, "I will not let bitterness define me."

The virtuous woman is not defined by perfection, but by her persistence in love. Her nobility shines brightest in adversity. She rises early, not because she must, but because love wakes her. She extends her hands to the poor, not because she has plenty, but because grace has made her generous.

When she forgives the unforgivable and feeds the one who once wounded her, she mirrors the mercy of Heaven. Her worth cannot be measured in rubies, because her value is not in what she possesses — but in who she has become through surrender.

Her friend could not understand her compassion, but Heaven recorded it as righteousness. She did not respond out of naivety, but out of revelation — "Because I was him."

That is divine faithfulness — to love redemptively, to act mercifully, to give grace as freely as it was given to you.

Meditative Reflection

Think of someone who hurt you deeply.
Now imagine God standing between you both,
pouring mercy into your hands.
Whisper, "Because I was them."
Let grace become your response.

Affirmation Prayer

El Rachum, the God of Compassion,
Make me faithful as You are faithful.
Let mercy flow through me like a river of healing.
Teach me to love when it costs me, to forgive when it hurts
me,
and to reflect Your heart in every act of grace.
In the matchless Name of Yeshua, Amen.

Wisdom Key

Virtue is not proven by comfort, but by compassion in conflict.

End of Week
Reflection

"He that walketh uprightly walketh surely…"
Proverbs 10:9

This week has shown us that righteousness is not a momentary choice, but a lifelong path—a path illuminated step by step by the faithfulness of God. The light that began as a faint glow has grown stronger with every obedient step, every courageous stand, every quiet act of integrity.

We have learned that righteousness produces boldness—not the bravado of self-confidence, but the courage that flows from knowing we are covered, called, and kept by God. The righteous do not flee because they are not hiding. They stand firm because truth has made them free.

Integrity revealed itself as a generational gift. A just life does more than bless the present—it prepares the future. Every honest decision, every unseen act of faithfulness, becomes a path others can walk safely upon. Righteousness leaves footprints of peace for those who follow.

We also encountered the beauty of faithfulness—the kind that loves when it would be easier to withdraw, that gives when it would be justified to withhold, that responds with mercy instead of memory. In that faithfulness, we glimpsed the very heart of God, who loved us not because we deserved it, but because He is righteous.

By the end of this week, one truth stands radiant: the rewards of righteousness are not merely external. They are inward and eternal—clarity instead of confusion, peace instead of fear, courage instead of retreat, legacy instead of loss. The light does not fade; it intensifies. The closer we walk with God, the clearer the way becomes.

So we pause here—not in exhaustion, but in gratitude.
We look back and see how far the light has carried us.
We look ahead and trust that it will only grow brighter.

Keep walking, beloved.
The path you are on is leading you somewhere holy.
And the light that guides you will not dim—
it will shine more and more, until the perfect day.

Selah

The Journey of Wisdom Continues

"Wisdom is the principal thing; therefore get wisdom: and
with all thy getting get understanding."
— Proverbs 4:7 (KJV)

Thirty-one days have passed.

Thirty-one windows of divine revelation opened before your
soul.

You have walked the narrow path with Solomon and stood at
the crossroads of choice,

listening for the whisper of Wisdom.

She has not shouted; she has sung.

Her song is steady, timeless — a melody calling you back to
reverence, back to trust, back to the fear of the Lord.

You have listened.

You have reflected.

You have prayed.

But the journey of wisdom does not end here — it begins
again each morning.

For wisdom is not a destination; it is a rhythm.

It breathes in every act of kindness,

moves in every decision rooted in truth,

and shines in every step that walks humbly with God.

Let the words of Proverbs now become the way of your life.

Let understanding dwell richly in your heart.

Let discernment guide your hands,

and may your days be filled with the peace that only Heaven can give.

Walk in wisdom.

Speak with grace.

Love with depth.

Forgive freely.

And remember this:

Every act of faithfulness, every quiet obedience, every humble choice —

becomes a verse in the living book of your legacy.

When others read your life, may they see wisdom alive within you.

And when your journey ends, may Heaven's pages record this testimony:

"They walked with God — and were found faithful."

Selah

A Prayer of Forgiveness, Restoration, Renewal, and Thanksgiving

"Create in me a clean heart, O God;
and renew a right spirit within me."

— Psalm 51:10 (KJV)

Eternal Father,

God of mercy, grace, and unfailing love —

I come before You humbled, grateful, and aware of how deeply I need You.

You have been patient when I was restless,

faithful when I was frail,

and gracious when I was guilty.

Even when I strayed, Your love followed me into the far country

and waited for my return.

Forgive me, Lord, for every word, deed, and thought

that grieved Your Spirit or dimmed Your light within me.

Wash me again in the blood of the Lamb.

Cleanse the hidden places of my soul

and renew a steadfast spirit within me.

Let Your mercy rewrite my memories

and Your grace reclaim every broken place.

Restore my joy, O God.

Revive my passion for Your presence.

Let the oil of gladness replace every spirit of heaviness,

and let peace once again reign in the chambers of my heart.

Breathe new life into my calling,

and awaken the dreams You planted before the foundation of the world.

I release every offense and every offender.

I choose forgiveness — freely, completely, joyfully.

For how can I cling to bitterness when You have forgiven me of so much?

Heal the wounds that unforgiveness left behind,

and fill me with compassion that overflows.

Now, Lord, I turn my heart toward thanksgiving.

Thank You for loving me through every season —

for the mountain peaks and the valley floors,

for the answered prayers and the waiting rooms,

for every delay that turned out to be divine.

Thank You for mercy new every morning,

for grace that never runs dry,

for wisdom that continues to whisper when the world grows loud.

I thank You for every lesson hidden in loss,

for every friend who walked beside me,

for every tear that watered the seeds of faith.

Thank You for the cross that redeemed me,

the blood that restored me,

and the Spirit that renews me daily.

You have been my refuge and my reward,

my portion and my peace.

All that I am and all that I have belong to You.

Let my restored life bring You glory,

let my renewed heart reflect Your love,

and let my grateful soul never forget Your goodness.

Today, I stand forgiven, restored, renewed — and deeply thankful.

From this day forward, I will live as one redeemed by grace

and sustained by gratitude.

In the matchless, merciful, and mighty Name of

Yeshua HaMashiach — my Redeemer, my Restorer, my Renewal, and my Reward —

Amen.

About the Author
Aaron Maxwell Montgaue

Aaron M. Montague, MBA, MDiv, PNLP, PTT, CCHt, CSC

Aaron M. Montague is a preacher, strategist, and builder of people who believes that ordinary folks—when united by vision, discipline, and love—can create extraordinary change. As the visionary mind behind the West Philadelphia Billionaires Society (WPBS), he champions a bold, simple idea: one million people, one dollar a day, building community-owned wealth that cannot be outsourced, gentrified away, or stolen by neglect.

A retired U.S. Armed Forces veteran with over twenty-one years of combined service in the Army and Navy, Aaron learned leadership, discipline, and sacrifice the hard way—under pressure, under orders, and often under commitment. After military retirement, he continued serving others as a certified Veterans Appeals advocate with a nationally recognized Veterans Service Organization, fighting to ensure that those who bore the battle receive the care and benefits they earned. That same warrior spirit now fuels his fight for economic justice, neighborhood ownership, and generational prosperity.

Aaron is the founder of Montague Motivational Ministries (MX3), where he blends his training in business (MBA), theology (MDiv), and transformational change (PNLP, PTT, CCHt, CSC) to empower believers, leaders, and everyday people to renew their minds, heal their stories, and rebuild their financial foundations. As a life coach, Bible teacher, and trance therapist, he speaks to both the conscious and subconscious mind—challenging limiting beliefs while igniting faith, vision, and action.

At the heart of Aaron's work is a simple conviction: we are not powerless, and we are not for sale. Through WPBS, he casts a prophetic, practical blueprint for turning scattered dollars into concentrated power—investing in gas stations, mini-marts, housing, healthcare, education, and more, all under community ownership. His writing weaves Scripture, street-level wisdom, financial literacy, and a fierce love for Black and Brown communities into a call-to-action that is as spiritual as it is strategic.

Aaron is a husband, father, grandfather, mentor, and spiritual coach to many. Whether he is preaching in a pulpit, coaching leaders in a boardroom, or sketching out community investment models on a napkin, his message remains the same: You were not born just to survive in someone else's system. You were created to build, own, and steward the Kingdom impact God has placed in your hands.

The West Philadelphia Billionaires Society is more than a book to him—it is a blueprint, a battle plan, and a love letter to communities that have been overlooked, underestimated, and under-capitalized for far too long.

To correspond with or book the author for speaking engagments, please contact him at:

aaron@mx3motivational.com

- or for more books from the author -

Visit his online bookstore:

http://MX3Motivationalbooks.com

www.ingramcontent.com/pod-product-compliance
Lightning Source LLC
Chambersburg PA
CBHW051223120626
46547CB00013B/1483